HOW YOU BEGAN

AMABEL WILLIAMS-ELLIS

Illustrated by JOHN BARBER

When you had been growing for about a fortnight, you were about as big as this capital O or a grain of rice. You looked rather like a short lumpy worm, but it didn't seem that you had finished — it looked as if you were still changing. It seemed as if the cells somehow knew that a worm wasn't the sort of creature you were going to grow into.

Tiny bits of you began to grow and push out; there was one at the top end of you, two at the other end, and two at the sides. What were these little knobs going to be?

Find out how YOU began and also how all the animals around us have developed from tiny blobs of jelly that were the first living things on the Earth many millions of years ago.

3bcd

HOW YOU BEGAN

A CAROUSEL BOOK 0 552 54064 1

First published in Great Britain
by Gerald Howe Ltd.

PRINTING HISTORY
Gerald Howe edition published 1928
Carousel revised and updated edition published 1975

Carousel Books are published by Transworld Publishers, Ltd,
Cavendish House, 57–59 Uxbridge Road, Ealing, London W.5

Printed in Great Britain by James Paton Ltd., Gordon Street, Paisley, Scotland.

ACKNOWLEDGEMENT

Acknowledgement is made to the following for permission to reproduce photographs: Popperfoto; The Zoological Society of London; Amabel Williams-Ellis.

The 'Afterwords' by Professor J. B. S. Haldane were added by way of endorsement to the original edition of 1928. The present edition has been revised with the help of Dr. M. Pearson, research student in comparative neuroanatomy.

HOW YOU BEGAN

YOU were once a tiny speck of jelly. This was months before you became a baby or were born. You had no hands, or feet, or arms or legs or head.

You had no mouth, or eyes; you were smaller than a pin's head, or the full stop of this page, quite soft, and almost round.

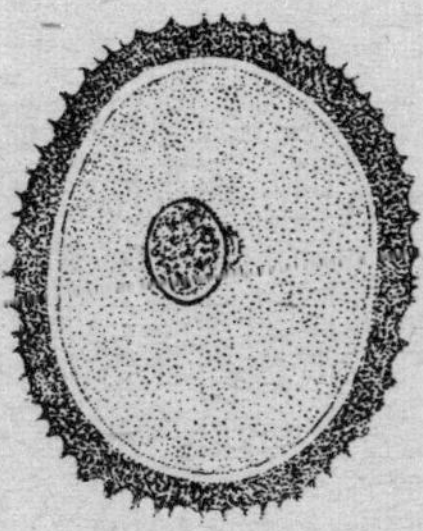

Fig. 2 — When you began you were only as big as the dot in the middle or as one of the full stops on this page.

You did not like anything or hate anything, or feel glad or sorry.

Only you always meant to grow. Growing was a thing you somehow had to do.

You know how, when a person is asleep in bed, if the sheet or blanket gets pulled over their nose so that they can't breathe comfortably, they wriggle or push the bedclothes away without waking up?

That was just the way in which you wanted to grow. You had to grow, just as the person who is asleep has to breathe. Wanting to grow is so strong that a plant that wants to grow will move away a stone that stops it from pushing out of the ground.

But for a long time you, the little speck of jelly, went on growing without waking up, just as a person goes on quietly breathing all night.

* * *

Once, long ago, it seems that there were no proper animals, or fish, or insects, in the world, only little spots of jelly smaller than pins' heads, and not nearly so tidy and round. There were, at first, no creatures in the world except this kind, which was very much like you when you began.

There are still plenty of such tiny, nearly shapeless creatures about, only they are too small to see.

Some of them float about in the water and they have no eyes, or arms, or legs or flippers or suckers. They can't move about very far or even stay still; they mostly float where the winds or the tides, or the streams, take them. If the water is still, they can manage to get along a tiny bit by a sort of rolling and stretching, but moving water carries thousands of these tiny things along. They can't do anything to stop themselves. Some live in salt water and some in fresh, they are animals, not plants, and eat very tiny bits of sea-weed or pond-weed that get broken off whatever is growing near, or else they eat tiny green plants that float about just as they do.

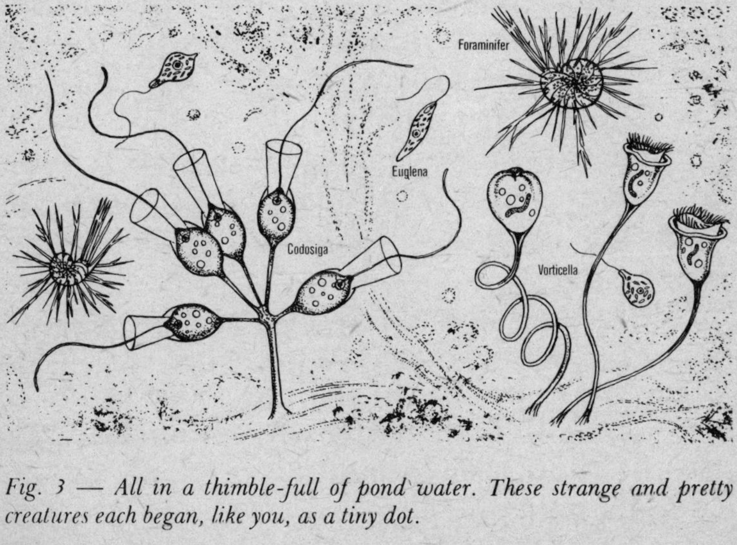

Fig. 3 — All in a thimble-full of pond water. These strange and pretty creatures each began, like you, as a tiny dot.

But they can't see, and they can't swim, so they have to wait till they happen to float near a scrap of food. When that happens the tiny jelly-creature opens itself anywhere and swallows the food. They don't have a special mouth or special stomach. You could see for yourself how they manage if you were to take a bit of plasticine or clay, and then dent it in anywhere and wrap it round a pebble or a nut or a small marble. If you try this you will have made a model, only bigger, of how the first creatures in the world ate their meals.

But the first jelly-creatures were ever so much smaller than your bit of plasticine or clay and, if you go on with this book, you will find out why they had to be so small.

But, as you will have guessed, very often these very small creatures don't happen to bump into a bit of food. Sometimes the tide or the stream floats them up on to the land and leaves them there, high and dry on the beach or the bank of the stream. Then there is nothing to float in. So after they have eaten anything that they happen to be touching, they get no more food.

Bits of food might often be quite close in the water or on the land. If only the poor creatures could have seen or smelt a little, and swum, or wriggled a little bit better, they could have got the food. But they couldn't.

So then they died.

Heaps and heaps of such tiny creatures die because they can't see, or swim, or wriggle enough to get at a crumb of food. It's great waste. This sort of waste went on for thousands and millions of years and it goes on still, for there are millions and millions of such tiny creatures to this day. There really are far more of them than there are of us or of bigger animals, only they are so small that people forget about them.

* * *

Now each of these jelly-creatures, like everything else that is alive, has always wanted to live and to grow. It does not want, in the way you might want a book, or want to look at television or to go out. It wants in the way you want to breathe — must breathe — even when you are asleep. The tiny creatures have always wanted to stay alive. They have wanted this all the time, just as you wanted to grow when you were only a little jelly-creature, and like the first live creatures that ever were on earth.

There was one great difference, though, between you and the first live creatures. It took thousands of millions of tiny jelly-creatures living for millions of years, for a few of them to be able, little by little, to see their food, or to be able to smell it, and to grow flippers or fins or a sort of whiplash arrangement so as to move to get something to eat. But a lot of them never changed, and so, as well as the sorts in the picture, there are plenty of other ordinary kinds of tiny jelly-creatures to this day. But till you can use a microscope you won't be able to see them for yourself. Microscopes were used to make all the drawing or photographs of them that are in this and other books, in films or on television.

But you can see something that is very like them if you look at a frog's egg, which is big enough to see. Looking at a frog's egg — the middle part, not the jelly — is very much like looking at the first creatures down a microscope, except that the frog's egg is neater and rounder as well as being a lot bigger.

Fig. 4 — This is a tadpole, so small you could only just see it, but it's nearly hatched out of its jelly-egg.

And what about you when you began? You too looked very much like the frog's egg, but though you have grown to be ever so much bigger than even the biggest sort of frog, you were once ever so much smaller than a frog's egg.

* * *

You grew — as all living creatures do — in a special way, which is not like stretching a bit of elastic or blowing up a balloon. Instead of growing much bigger the tiny jelly that was you, grew just a little and then it began to divide. Then each half-jelly grew to be as big as the first jelly. Then each of the new ones divided again. One, two, four, eight, sixteen, thirty-two and so on.

It was like this:

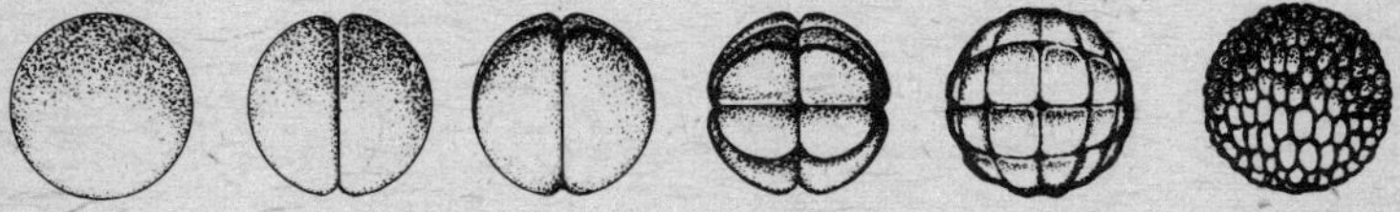

Fig. 5 — You were still very tiny, but growing: one cell split into two, and then each cell split again.

But even after dividing had begun, you were still very small, and no particular shape.

Then, as you grew, you began to change. The little jelly-lumps out of which you are made were getting not to be exactly like each other. It seemed as if they might be going to be part of something. There seemed to be an inside part of this something, and a middle part, and an outside part.

After a while, though you were still too small to see, you got a bit longer. Then a sort of dent seemed to come all down you and you began to fold. This was a great change! You really had done something. Now, at the end of about a fortnight, you were a fairly long-shaped, hollow tube of jelly.

But you were still tiny and you had no arms or legs or head, and you were made of tiny little jelly-lumps (called cells) just as walls are made of bricks or stones.

Each little bit of you was still growing on its own, and there still wasn't much difference between one part of you and another.

* * *

Just as there are still tiny jelly-lumps that are too small to see, there are, as well, to this day, creatures that stay at this small long-shaped stage.

For instance, there are small wormy things called flat-worms. They are really rather grander than you were then, and can do more than you could. But their cells are much more alike than the cells of a creature with bones and hair or feathers. If you cut a flat-worm in two, each bit will grow the missing half again so that then there are two small flat-worms instead of one bigger one. Perhaps being cut in two hurts? It's hard to tell, but the two small flat-worms seem to go on all right.

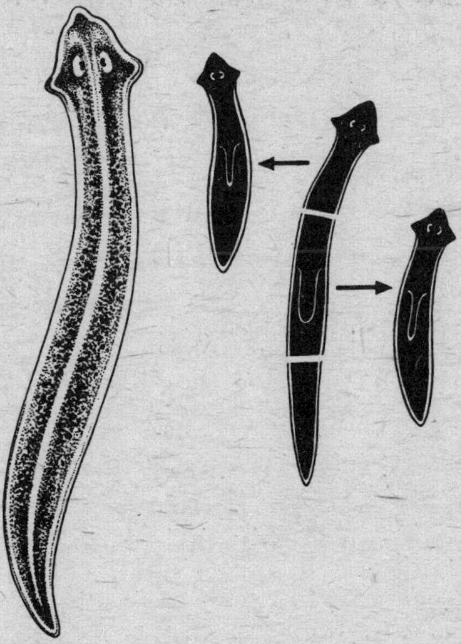

Fig. 6 — Flat-worms are so small that they are hard to see. If you cut one into three pieces, the head end would grow a new tail and the tail end would grow a new head.

Of course an animal like a rabbit or a cat would die if it got cut in half in a road accident. With the worm there isn't one bit which really is the worm and one bit which isn't. But suppose a man's legs were cut off in an accident, or a kangaroo's tail? A man could live without his legs, and a kangaroo without her tail, but his legs couldn't live without him, nor could her tail without her, and, as you know very well, it would be the same if a dog or a cat were run over and a paw or a leg got cut off.

There are bits of any of the bigger animals, a cat a mouse, or a person, that are no good without the rest; paws, tails and hands are very useful to the cat or man for clawing, climbing, waving, or holding tea-cups. But they are not the cat or the man, and they can't live without the cat's or the man's brain to tell them when to wave, and what to hold.

But flat-worms and a few other sorts of creatures are nearly the same all over, just as you once were. They are not very clever and can't hear, or run or think very well, but they can grow missing parts again.

* * *

When you had been growing for about a fortnight, with this cell splitting going on all the time, you were about as big as this capital o or a grain of rice.

All baby animals grow by their cells dividing like that. And with some creatures you can see some of it happen. Frogs lay jelly-eggs in the shallow parts of ponds. Each egg looks like a clear jelly with a black spot and, if you are patient and have a good look every day, you can see all this happening fairly well before the black spot turns into a tadpole. You can't see the separate cells dividing, they are too small, but you can see that parts of the black spot are turning into different parts of what is going to be a tadpole.

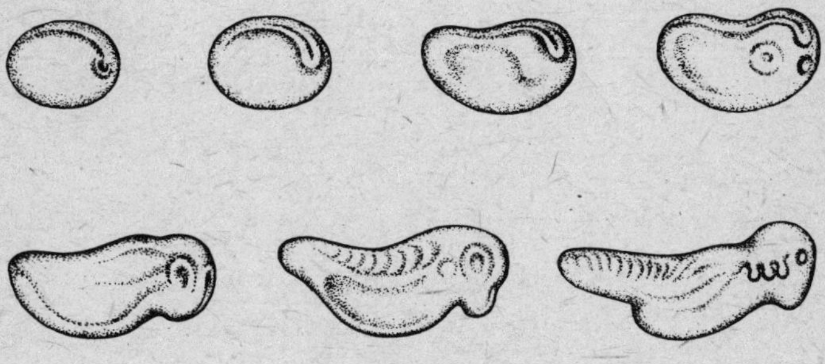

Fig. 7 — Here are the stages that a tadpole goes through before it becomes a frog. The stripes are going to be gills for breathing in water.

When you were about as big as a grain of rice and were rather like a short lumpy worm, it didn't seem that you had finished — it looked as if you were still changing. It seemed as if the cells somehow knew that a worm wasn't the sort of creature you were going to grow into.

Tiny bits of you began to grow and push out; there was one at the top end of you, two at the other end, and two at the sides.

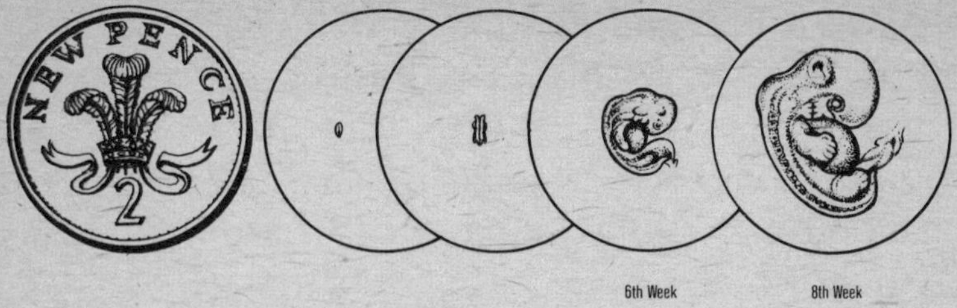

Fig. 8 — Notice how small you were at first. But you soon got a lot bigger than a tadpole.

What were these five little knobs going to be? Hard to say! But after about another week it seemed as if the top one was turning into a head.

Whose head? Was it going to be a sheep's head or a fish's head? That wasn't easy to say either. It was a big head for anyone as small as you still were, and it was bent down. Two eyes seemed to be growing in it. What about the rest of you? Had anything else happened to help at making a guess at what sort of creature you were turning into? It had.

* * *

You had folded, and you were fairly hollow. It was plain that the hollow was going to be some creature's inside, and also it seemed that where the fold had come, the jelly-lumps — the cells — were harder. In fact a hollow stick of soft bendable bone was growing all down you.

Well, that little soft stick showed one or two things. It was certain that you were not going to turn into a crab, a lobster, a starfish, or a spider, because you had begun to grow a backbone.

* * *

None of those creatures have backbones. Crabs and lobsters wear their bones outside them. We and rabbits, and all the furry and feathery creatures wear our bones inside.

As for real jellyfish and worms and slugs, they don't have any bones. That must be a great bother for any land animal, unless it is very small. Bones are most useful whether you wear them inside like a cat, or outside like a crab.

Fig. 9 — If you had no bones you would fall down in an untidy heap like this rag doll.

How difficult it would be to do anything if your arms and legs, or your back, had no bones in them! Your arms would only be like bits of rope, all floppy — and so would your legs — they would be of no use to walk on, and you, if you had no backbone, would be more like a pillow than a person.

But even when you had grown a backbone, there are lots of things that you seemed as if you might be going to turn into.

For one thing, at the end of four weeks you had got a tail. Could you be going to be a lamb? Or perhaps a pig? Those other four little short bits that stuck out — lower down than the head bit — might have been going to turn into legs, with hoofs at the end, or into paws or else perhaps flippers. In fact you didn't yet seem very much like a person, especially as you had that short neat tail — rather like a rabbit's tail.

Or could you be going to turn into a fish? That seemed rather a likely idea, for these little leggy things would have done nicely for fins and most fish have tails.

There was one other thing about you that made it seem that a fish was something you might grow into. For what is the biggest difference between a water beast and a land beast?

* * *

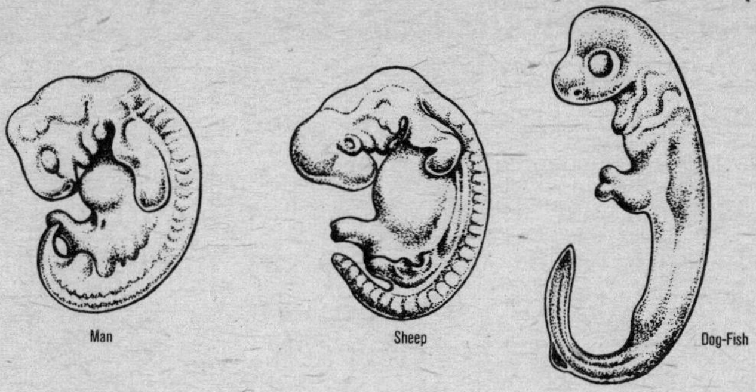

Fig. 10 — Could you tell, if they weren't marked, which of these embryos was going to turn into a person?

If you think of a fish and a land beast that look very much like each other, there is one big difference. An eel and a snake look very much alike. But an eel is a kind of fish and so it can breathe under water, but a snake drowns if it is under water for too long.

Every snake has a nose and lungs, and a nose and lungs are no good for breathing under water. Underwater creatures such as eels and fish have gills instead.

Well, what was happening to you as you grew? You began to grow slits in your neck that looked as if they were all ready to become the openings for gills. For about a fortnight you seemed to setting to work to grow gills, just as though you were going to be a fish.

There were other things about you that were also like a fish. One of these was your heart.

Nowadays, like other good-sized land animals (horses, or sheep, mice and so on) you have quite a grand heart to pump your blood. It is more or less heart-shaped and if you are now about eight or ten years old it is about as big as your fist. It has tubes leading to it called veins, and tubes leading away from it called arteries, and it has four parts to it — with one-way swing doors between each pair.

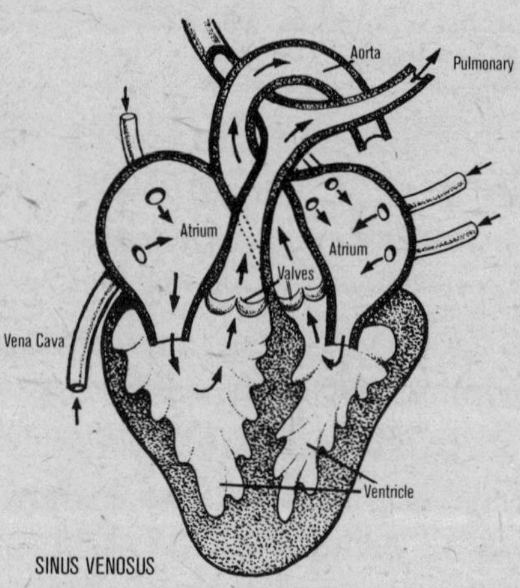

Fig. 11 — A mammal's heart. You've got one; a complicated pump. You can hear it if you listen.

Without thinking about it, you keep squeezing up first one side of your heart and then the other. At your age you do this at nearly a hundred times a minute. One squeeze of the left side pumps fresh clean blood through long tubes round to places like your toes and your head (to feed them) and a squeeze of the other side pumps used blood to your lungs for freshening up with another lot of air. It is all very well arranged, with different parts of your heart doing different things.

A fish has long tubes like yours for blood, and in one of these (which is rather like a thin bit of rubber piping) there is a much simpler heart than yours, not much more than a swelled out bit of the main tube. The fish (without thinking) squeezes this, and the squeeze just pushes the blood along past the gills where it is cleaned.

Well, in those days your heart wasn't as grand as it is now. It was more like a fish's heart, just a swelled-out bit of tube with no different parts, except one-way swing doors to prevent the blood going backwards.

So do you think it looked as if you were going to be a person? With a heart like that, and the beginning of gills to breathe under water with, and a tail?

Time would show! You were still very small, still not much bigger than a bean, you were still a bit of jelly that looked as if it might be going to turn into a fish.

But in a way (I'll try to explain this part better later) all these funny ideas about what you might turn into were like a sort of game or acting. You were really set to turn into a person, rather in the way that a gramophone record is set to play one particular bit of music, but you did look very much like a fish or an unborn pig. This stage went on for quite a long time before you began slowly to yawn, and stretch, and wake up enough to be born.

You and other mammals, such as pigs, goats or puppies, before they are ready to be born, all look as if they had been copying, in a sort of dream, changes that have taken hundreds of millions of years.

PART II

Long, long ago, when the earth we live on was quite different from what it is now, a few of the living creatures — the tiny jelly-creatures — had begun to change (several hundred million years ago or so people think) but this changing had not only been slow but very chancy. Millions upon millions of creatures changed in ways that turned out to be no good, and so those kinds died out.

This was so long ago that Earth had different seas and different land. Only the sun and the moon were about the same. But, in that far away time, being alive at all (instead of being a rock or some water) was something new and strange.

After a while the very first, smallest, kinds of

living creature began not only to change, but to grow bigger. Their ways of growing bigger, however, weren't like blowing up a balloon, any more than your dream way had been.

You remember that the very smallest floating Jelly-creatures (single-celled creatures) looked and still look rather like this:

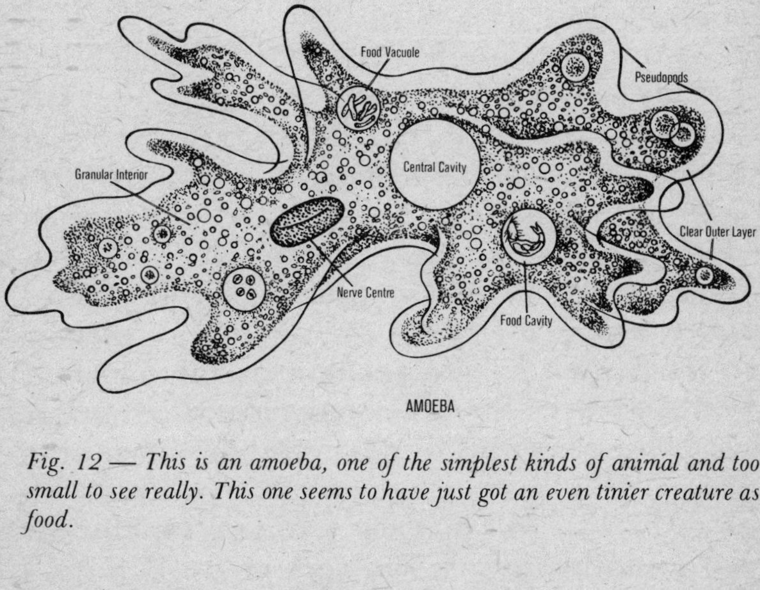

Fig. 12 — This is an amoeba, one of the simplest kinds of animal and too small to see really. This one seems to have just got an even tinier creature as food.

Just as you did, these tiny creatures still begin to grow by each cell dividing and turning into two cells. Then these two cells each grew big enough to split and so on. This was exactly how you yourself began to grow. But then came a difference. At first when one cell turned into two cells, the new cells didn't stay together.

So instead of one, there were two separate creatures.

The beginnings of all the bigger animals in the world — such as you — came when the cells divided but kept together. Then instead of two very tiny creatures there was something just a little bigger, a bunch of cells all packed together. This was the beginning of tiny one-celled animals turning into a new sort of creature.

Some of their cells now did different jobs. For instance the cells on the outside of the cell-bunch got a bit harder than the others, so that they made a skin that kept out the water and dirt. Sometimes these cells grew harder than skin, in fact they grew into shells, so that bumping about didn't spoil the inside part so much.

When they had got a skin or a shell to protect them, some of the cells on the inside got better at melting up the bits of food. This was the beginning of having a stomach. A creature with a stomach could manage to digest tougher or harder food bits that had been no use before.

That seems to be the kind of way in which creatures that were made of more than just one cell, got a skin or a shell and then a tummy. Then they were more likely to stay alive because they didn't get damaged so much by bumping into things, and also they could use more of the food.

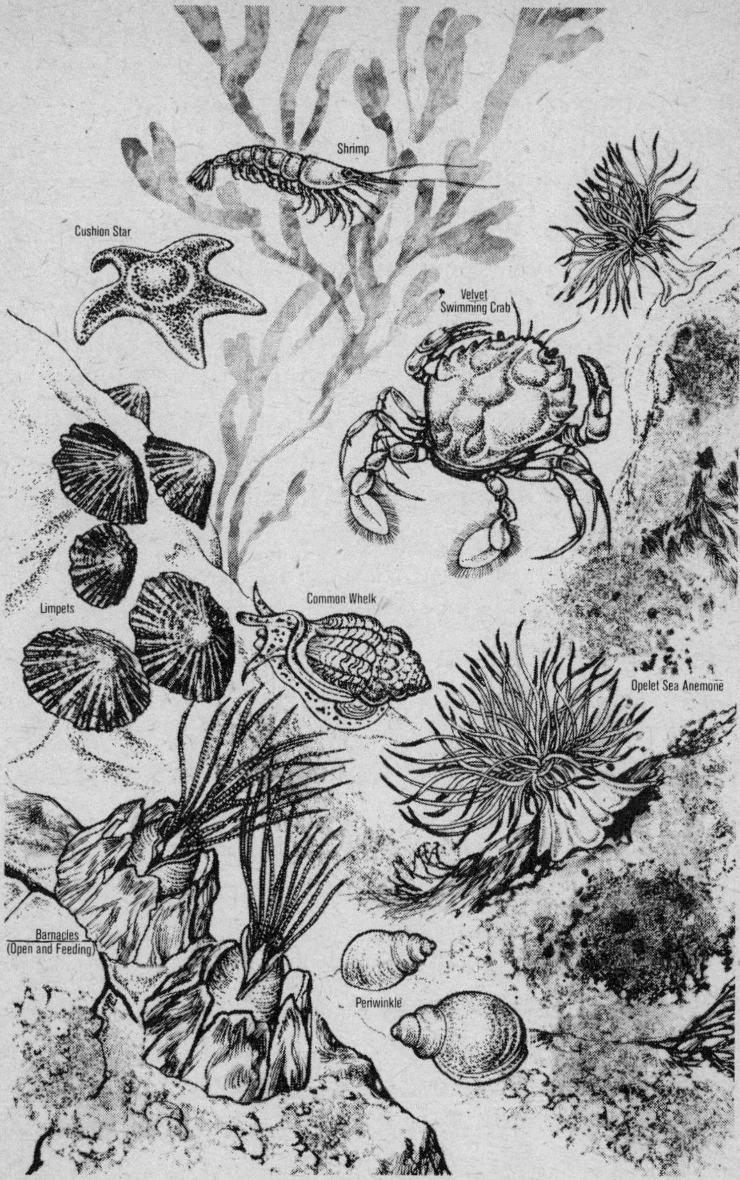

Fig. 13 — Some larger creatures wear their bones outside.

After a while creatures grew that also had all sorts of ways of moving. What they grew were not always legs or fins (look at the pictures).

But some creatures didn't bother with moving but grew suckers to prevent the tide or the wind from floating them away or banging them to bits against rocks.

There were of course no humans alive in those far-away times, so we don't know for sure just how the tiny creatures changed. These pictures are of creatures that are alive now. Some are made of just one tiny floating cell, some, though they are made of several cells, still have all their cells almost the same.

Some have just got a skin and a stomach, and a mouth in the skin, and a way in for food to get to the stomach. Some stick to one place with suckers, some can just wriggle about and some can move for a little way (but very fast) by thrashing about with things like whiplashes.

* * *

But as you can guess it isn't much good for a creature to be able to move about if it can't tell where to go. Quite a lot of these tiny things got to be able to do two things that you do with your nose and mouth, that is smell and taste. These were ways of telling where there are bits of food. Also they began to know about the things that your skin or nose or your tongue and the inside of your mouth tell you.

"This is horrible! Much too salt", your mouth tells you, if you happen to get a mouthful of sea water. Or "This is too hot" is what your skin tells you if you try putting your hand in very hot water — say a hot spring in New Zealand or Japan.

But, as you very well know, feeling and smelling aren't the only ways in which a person like you decides what to do. You, and nearly all the big creatures except the kinds that live in dark caves, look at things. Eyes are very important. Sometimes big creatures specially need to look at things a long way off — fast-running greyhounds and cheetahs do for instance. But some animals, such as monkeys and apes, are much better than cheetahs or greyhounds at looking carefully at something that is quite close. You, and also a monkey or a chimpanzee, often use both your hands and eyes for this. You often pick up a small thing and look at it carefully so as to decide what to do with it.

Most other animals can't do this. Even dogs and cats can't. And most of the very tiny creatures don't seem to be able to do much more than tell light from dark.

But there isn't just one best way to stay alive. There are hundreds and thousands of different creatures in the world now with different ways of smelling, feeling, hearing and seeing.

Fig. 14 — The boy is looking at a sea-urchin's shell. His dog and the sea-gull can't hold things and look at them. But they can see far-away things.

Perhaps weak ones as well as strong ones began some of the changes. This is just a guess. But suppose two jelly-creatures were tired of floating and being banged about. The stronger one's child and grand-child and great-great-great-grand-child would gradually grow beautiful paddles and whiskers and a fringed tail and become a shrimp. But perhaps the weak one's children would grow suckers, to hang on to the rocks with, and perhaps a shell as well and lead a very quiet life and be a barnacle. Anyhow, we do know two things for certain about the beginning of animal life on earth. First, that changes took a very long time — it took millions of years — to get all the changes from the first live creatures with only one cell, to an elegant little fish with bones, and scales, and tubes for blood, and a stomach for digesting, and eyes to see with, and gills to breathe in water with and beautiful colours as well.

Second, there were almost certainly fish before there were any land animals. So that you, when you rather looked as if you might be going to be a fish, were doing just what the creatures in the beginning of life on earth did.

Changing had once been grim earnest, where lots of creatures died because they changed too quickly or else not quickly enough. Millions and millions never changed at all, and millions and millions even changed backwards, and forgot how to grow shells or suckers or fins.

Only a few creatures, of all the millions alive at any one time in the history of the earth, managed to grow up and have children and pass on to them the changes that have got us, and all the other living animals, to being the sort of creatures we are now. You and all the other baby mammals just acted the real story over to yourself in a kind of play, where everything went right.

PART III

We said at the end of page 000 that, when you had been growing for about four weeks, you did not look as if you were very likely to become a person because of your tail and your gill-slits. You hadn't yet got real eyes or ears, and there was not all that much difference between your head, your neck, and your body. However your arms and legs were getting on.

By the end of another week your short stubby knobs of arms and legs would bend in the middle, at the places where your knees and elbows are now. You were growing a nose and lungs too, but you didn't quite throw away the slits for your gills but kept them a little longer as if they might come in useful. They weren't real grown-up fish's gills, not good enough to use in real water, and at that stage you hadn't got proper nostrils either, but only dents that didn't lead anywhere.

You were certainly going to have eyes though. In fact, for your size, your eyes were fairly big, but they were only made of a sort of puckered skin. You hadn't yet got a beautiful hard eyeball or lids and lashes and there were no pretty colours. You grew all these afterwards.

When you had been growing for about five weeks, you were still very small indeed and either you or I might easily have been mistaken for a pig at the same stage. (Not for a grown-up pig of course.)

You had got one lot of joints in your arms and one lot in your legs. All your bones were still very soft but your backbone was the best.

It looked as if there might still be a chance that your arms and legs would turn into flippers, and that you might grow up to be a seal, and swim in the sea, or flop about on the rocks, and have beautiful long whiskers and bark like a rather hoarse dog.

By now, however, it was clear you were not going to be any sort of fish, because you were growing lungs and a nose for breathing air.

Your tummy and heart were getting on, too.

A person has a very grand inside for digesting food — a stomach and intestines and so on. It has all sorts of pipes and tubes in it, and a regular factory goes on working all the time — day and night — for getting all sorts of things that you need out of the food you have eaten. But your inside is still very much like a pig's or a seal's or a cat's. But after five weeks it wasn't quite like a grass-eating animal's inside.

* * *

What were you like after you had grown for a bit longer? Say for about eight weeks? You were still extremely small, not as big as a table-tennis ball, not much bigger, in fact, than a good-sized horse-chestnut.

A few more things were clear about you. You were not going to have hoofs for you had begun to have fingers and toes. But your short tail had not quite disappeared. (It's still there but it's tucked in now so that you seem as if you haven't got one.)

So after about eight weeks of growing and changing it was sure that you were not going to be a goat, a pig, a sheep or a deer, but would turn into some sort of creature with paws, or else hands and feet; and the way your inside was arranged meant that you were not going to live on grass.

Also by now you had got eyelids (fish don't have them) and the beginnings of a nose.

* * *

I wonder if you have thought of a thing which the growing cells in your body had always been set to do? The jelly-creatures, long, long ago, had had to see about it almost as soon as some of their cells began to do one sort of work and some another.

It was this. You needed telegraph wires.

Why? When the outer cells of a tiny jelly-creature turned into skin, and the inner cells turned into a tummy and the creature could see and move about a little, a way of sending messages was needed. Tummy wanted more to eat, and wanted the fins or flippers to try to go where there was some food. A sort of feeling, a hungry feeling, came through from tummy:

"You bit that can move us about! Please get busy!"

"All right!" said the creeping bit or the flippers. So off the creature paddled or crept, and, with luck, some food was found: then the outer part told tummy to get ready to digest, and then it swallowed or else it just folded round the bit of food.

Gradually the parts through which these feelings came and went got better at passing on the news.

Eyes, ears and smelling parts got better and so there began to be more and more messages — feeling messages, smelling messages, and hearing and seeing messages.

When a living creature gets to be as grand as a fish, with different parts doing different things, a kind of post office grows up and a special thinking, choosing part as well.

The thinking and choosing part of you, (or of a puppy) is, as you know, the brain. The message-taking parts (which are like long white threads) are called nerves, and they work rather like telegraph or telephone wires.

You don't think with your toes, nor does a cat nor a kangaroo think with its tail. But toes and tails have telegraph wires — nerves — which take and send messages.

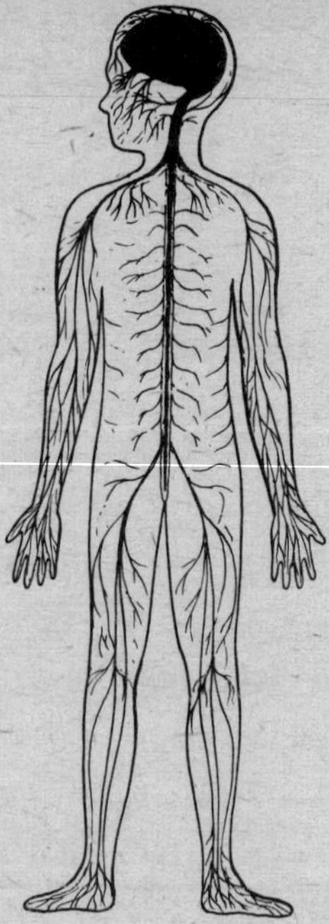

Fig. 15 — Your telegraph wires. Notice that there are more to your hands and fingers so you can feel things best with these.

You began to get nerves ready by the time you had cells doing separate jobs — skin, tummy, hands, eyes, nose and so on — because soon, when it was time for you to be born, there would be a lot of messages.

It is a good thing for a creature to have its telegraph lines kept very safe. (Look at the picture). If something went wrong with yours you would not know that your toe or your finger were being burnt, or nibbled by a rat,

SOME OF THE STRANGE CREATURES THAT HAVE DEVELOPED

The Warthog

The Toucan

The Thick-Tailed Bushbaby and young

The Vampire Bat

The Octopus

The Furry Armadillo

The Wallaby and her young

The author and her cat
Alexander Pushkin

and that you must quickly do something about it.

A big animal, such as you or a dog, can't do without nerves. The smell-nerves in his nose say to a dog: "There's a delicious bit of meat not far from me", and, quick as winking, brain flashes a message back to his teeth, tongue and throat:

"Snap it up and swallow it!" If you are friends with a dog you can try, and you'll see how fast all that can be done. Fish's brains and nerves are also very quick at this sort of thing, and so are birds'.

* * *

But there were once very large animals in the world — Dinosaurs, Iguanodons, Brontosauros, for instance. Some of them were simply enormous — as big as a cottage, much heavier than an elephant and taller than a giraffe. Now these big, heavy creatures had tiny brains. They probably only understood very slowly what was happening yards and yards away at the tips of their long tails — much more slowly than you know what's going on with your toes. Even when they did find out what it was their brains were so small that they were probably not much good at deciding what to do, and even when they had decided, the huge, silly creatures probably did it very slowly.

Brontosauros and Diplodocus ate grass and leaves by the ton, and if there was no grass or not enough leaves in the places where they generally found them, then they must often have been too slow and stupid to look for the tons of food they needed in other places. And so they died.

There were also huge creatures such as Tyrannosaurus that fought the huge slow beasts and then ate them, and there were also smaller, quicker creatures that very likely managed to get to the food first.

There were no people in the world then, so nobody can be quite sure what went on or why none of these prehistoric beasts are alive now. What is certain is that they did die out and these seem likely reasons. But we know for certain that there were once such creatures, because of their bones — odd huge bones. Whole skeletons have sometimes been found, as well as, now and again, their enormous eggs. It seems as if it hadn't been a good idea to be very stupid as well as very big, though very stupid smallish creatures have gone on living all right. There are still plenty of creatures such as oysters and mussels and slugs and worms that don't seem to be very bright. Most of these spend a great deal of their time hiding or holding on tight to rocks.

The bigger creatures — elephants — lions or you — that are alive now have been the ones

Fig. 16 — An Iguandon.

that were either clever, or quick, or both. Just being enormous, heavy and strong seems to have been no good.

* * *

You know a good deal about the cleverness of a great many creatures that arc alive today, birds, for instance; they build all kinds of nests, swallows and swifts fly far away to foreign countries when it is winter in the country where they were hatched. Blue-tits have learned how to peck the tops off milk-bottles to get the cream. Then there are sharp-eyed hawks and eagles, and gulls that fly high and strike suddenly.

It isn't only birds that do clever things; beavers make dams and houses for themselves, and gazelles and elephants have one or two gazelles or an elephant watching out while the rest feed. Most bears that live in snowy countries sleep warm all the winter.

Unless a creature is very small — just a few cells big — or decides just to cling to a rock, it had better be clever. All the strong, heavy dinosaurs, and the flying lizards with their frightful teeth and their wings like bats', are dead, and all their children are dead. But the sly fox, and the leopard that leaps as quick as fire, and the squirrel that lays up nuts for the winter are alive, and so are their children. And so is man. For man is the cleverest of all the creatures, and there seems to be no beast, nor heat, nor cold, that can conquer man.

* * *

PART IV

So brains to think with and nerves to carry messages are important and when you began to get to horse-chestnut size you busily grew your brain, for that was going to be more use to you than teeth or claws or wings.

Even the brain of a baby chicken before it comes out of the egg is big, for its size, even though grown up cocks and hens are such silly creatures. In fact if you looked inside a hatching chicken's egg you would find that the chicken's head is nearly as big as the rest of its body. But as for YOUR head, it was, for your size, immense.

The brains of all the cleverer animals — dogs, cats, gorillas, elephants and so on — are arranged in a very good way.

You use one part of your brain for real thinking and choosing, while another part does the easier things and works on its own, so that the real thinking part is not bothered. You do this all the time and so does a cat.

Imagine that your cat is walking in a garden. Pretend that she has just had a saucer of milk, also that she is a mother cat, and has got kittens.

As your cat walks in this garden, the two parts of her brain are both working. The part of it that works of itself is quietly looking after her tummy and making it digest the milk she has just had. It is making sure that it is being turned into blood and bone and also cat's milk for the kittens, and also that she is being kept warm with it. This part of her brain is also seeing to her heart beats, moving her ribs as she breathes, and directing her four paws as she walks delicately over the grass. It is also probably gently twitching the very tip of her tail.

But her real thinking and choosing part is not bothering about any of these necessary things. Her choosing part is thinking (we will pretend) that too many people have come to

Fig. 17 — A mother cat will sometimes keep moving her kittens.

see her new kittens in their box in the kitchen, so she is deciding to carry them out, one by one, by the scruffs of their necks and take them to a quiet new place. Shall the new place be in a shed, in the garage, or in the broom cupboard? Which would be best? she is wondering.

It is just the same with you. Your real "You", your thinking, choosing brain, is not bothered by all the things that your body has to be doing all the time, such as digesting your meals, breathing, beating your heart and so on. You often do two or three things at once, without the least bother — you walk about, you whistle a tune, digest your breakfast — and all the time you can be thinking about whatever you like, about this book, or about a strange story that someone has told you, about football clubs or about something that you mean to make.

* * *

By the time you had been growing for about four months, you were still only about as big as a kitten that has just got its eyes open. Now there were only two things that you looked as if you might be going to be.

You couldn't be going to be a monkey because your tail had disappeared. Could you be going to be an ape? Or would you turn into a person? That was the question.

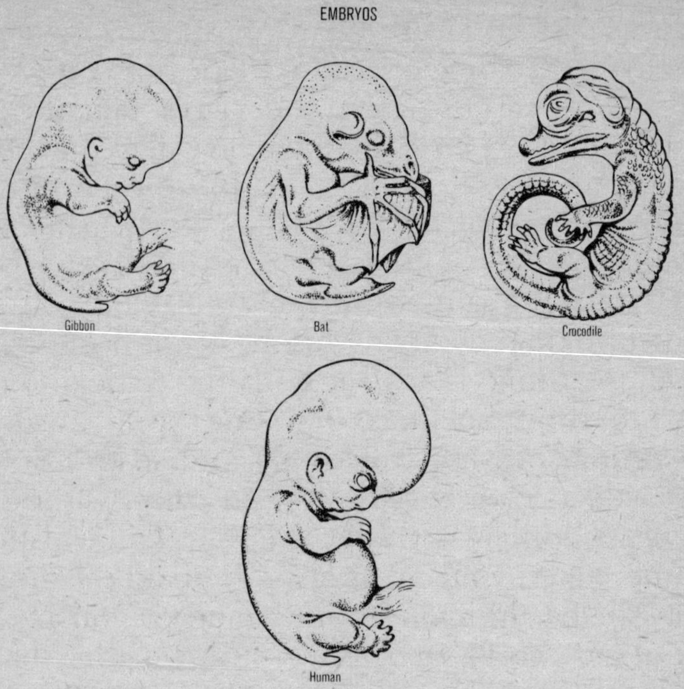

Fig. 18 — At last you can see which unborn creature is going to turn into a human. Or can you?

You could move a little, you had hands and feet. Your legs did not seem as if they were meant for very fast running, but they looked as if, later on, you would be able to do some running and climbing. You had definitely not got a strong lower jaw-bone for snapping and crunching like a wolf or a bear. To have really strong crunching jaws you must have a long-shaped, instead of a round head. But your head was round and your face was fairly flat. Your nose was short, and it was plain that it was not going to be as good for sniffing about as dog's. But your brain was big, like an ape's or person's.

You went on growing and when you had grown for five or six months, it was pretty certain that you were going to be a person, that's except for just one thing. Do you know what that one thing was?

When you had grown and changed for half a year you had a very neat coat of fine fluffy fur all over you — not just hair on your head. In fact you only really absolutely stopped playing at other creatures about six or eight weeks before you were ready to be born. You only shed that coat of hair when, at last, in every other way, you had become a human baby.

By then you had finished all your playing at the history of all the life on the whole earth.

You were ready to be a boy or a girl. You had left worm, fish, pig, dog and ape far away. And now, in a month, it would be time for you to be born.

You have often seen new babies and know a lot about the rest of the story of how a baby grows and learns; learns to see, to recognise people, both their faces and their voices, and in time to crawl, then to walk and to say words.

* * *

While you were changing and growing so quickly all the nine months before you were born you were really set to grow into a human baby. This seems to have been rather in the way a gramophone record is set to play the right music. But you can't tell what music it is going to be just by looking at the grooves on a record. In the same way unborn baby mammals look very much alike. However, cats never have puppies, and dogs never have kittens. A swan's egg never hatches into a goose, even if quite a lot of unborn creatures do look alike. We look so much alike because we are all related.

Perhaps you've noticed that, in all this book so far there hasn't been anything about where you were in those nine months? The fact is that humans, and all other mammals, have very special arrangements for rearing young ones safely. To grow each of the things that we mammals have got takes time — a skin, bones, sight, smell, nerves and a brain; for a human nine months, for a rat 22 days. But it took millions of years of failing and trying again and failing again. Many, many millions of baby creatures died of starvation, or of the cold, or were eaten, before these things worked properly.

Being a new kind of animal that was not quite finished, was generally more dangerous than being an old sort that did work all right, and many kinds of creature died out altogether.

But you were all right, and in no danger, you grew and changed every week or two, quite smoothly and gently. You were not too cold or too hot. The changing cells had all the food they needed for growing and splitting. Your whole dangerous changing and growing from a pin-head sized lump of jelly to a proper baby as big as a cat, only took you that nine months. You, like a puppy or a kitten, belong to the type of creature whose young change and grow in the safest possible place, that is, inside your mother, using the food she carried to you in her bloodstream.

All the long, long while, the thousands and thousands of years while so many creatures were very gradually changing, they were at the same time getting better ways of taking care of their children.

This was necessary because as they changed there were usually more and more bits to grow, so it took weeks or months for any baby creature to be like its father and mother. And all the time, while it was growing like them, it was blind and helpless, and could very easily get killed either by bad weather or by enemies.

Hundreds of kinds of creature that are alive now have hundreds of different ways of making sure that enough of their babies grow up.

One codfish for instance, lays several million eggs in the water. There are such a lot that enough of them are sure to live to grow up.

That's one way.

Birds have another way. Hens for instance, lay quite large eggs with hard shells. The tiny jelly part of a hen's egg, the part from which the chick really grows, is quite small. The rest of a hen's egg, or the egg of any other bird, is food for the growing chick. Outside it all — the food and the tiny jelly-egg — there is an egg-shell which protects it.

Fig. 19 — The hen is stepping delicately onto her nest. She will settle down and spread her wings over her eggs to keep them warm.

Often the father and mother birds build a nest and the hen bird lays her eggs in that. Then, either the mother, or both birds in turn, sit on the eggs to keep them warm. When at last the chicks are hatched, but can't fly, their parents fly and swim far and near to get food for them.

So with all this care, a great many baby birds

live to grow up, and there isn't half the waste of birds' eggs or of baby birds as there is of young fish or tadpoles.

* * *

But the furry animals — the mammals — have other ways. There is one great snag about birds' eggs. One of the two parents usually has to sit on them to keep them warm. This "sitting on the nest" often lasts for weeks till the eggs hatch. Then, if there are enemies about, the poor mother or father bird may get killed if they are found when they are sitting, or else, to save their own lives, they may have to fly away so that the eggs get cold or get eaten. However much the parent birds might like to, they can't take their eggs with them.

The plan that we mammals have is different. We have a safer place for babies. It is inside the mother. This has two big advantages. She can run away if enemies come, and also move about and get food. Her blood feeds her unborn baby and the warmth of her body keeps it warm.

Lambs are not born till they have grown a nice suit of wool to protect them, and long legs to run with. It is the same with a lot of other mammals — horses, donkeys, zebras, goats or giraffes, A few hours after it is born a foal, a lamb, a fawn or a kid, can run quite nicely, so that in a few hours their mothers can move about again, cropping the grass, and the babies can follow in a shakey sort of way. In a few days, if an enemy comes, the young ones can run well enough to keep near their mothers.

Fig. 20 — A mare and her foal.

But that is not the only care that a mammal mother takes of her young ones. She feeds them on her own milk for quite a long while. I expect you have seen this and how a sow, a mother cat, dog or cow, gives milk to her young ones. You can usually see plainly that she must be fond of them.

Most fish and frogs and insects do not bother with their children or take care of them at all. But nearly all feathered and furred creatures do bother a lot and so do humans. And because they are loved and taken care of, millions of the children of these creatures don't die like the frogs and fish.

It goes like this: first the mother has her child growing safe and warm in her body, then, when it is born, she gives it milk and loves it. Then later on she teaches it and helps it to learn. And all this her mother did for her, and if the baby is a girl, the baby will do the same for her children. If it is a boy and will grow into a mammal father — a human for instance — it might often help the mother in all sorts of ways in taking care and teaching the children for instance, and it is the father who gets the food for the mother and their young ones.

Fig. 21 — The man is trying to explain to the boys how a radio works.

A man does a lot of this. Nowadays he fetches iron and coal out of the earth, and oil and petrol to burn, and he has learned to make steam and water power and electricity work for him. And with the petrol, the oil, or the steam, he can go faster than the fastest horse, deer or ostrich and he flies further and higher than the eagle or the albatross — and even gets as far as the moon.

* * *

There is one question which used to puzzle me and may puzzle you. I don't think there is quite one whole answer to it, so that it still seems to me very odd. Anyhow, this is what I wanted to know when I was your age.

How does it happen that there are still so many absurd creatures in the world? (Turn back and take a good long look at the creatures whose photographs are on pages 000 and 000. We could have found many more, but that there wasn't room). Why are there still birds with things that look like coal-scuttles on their heads (such as toucans and hornbills) or cocks with tail feathers as long as a man, or birds with high fan-tails, such as peacocks?

Just think what it must be like to be one of the odd animals shown in the photographs. Surely some of those huge horns must be just a bother?

There ought, you might well think, to be some 'right' or 'best' way of changing? And yet the fact is that there are flamingoes, cats and humming birds, and us, and octopuses, and porcupines and zebras, and cockles and mussels, oysters and kangaroos and crocodiles and ever so many kinds of creatures that are too small to see, but that are very much alive to this day. You would have thought that there OUGHT to be just one, or at most two ways that were much the best for getting at your food and of keeping alive so that you could grow and have children?

This idea that there ought to be 'best ways' sounds like sense, but what you really FIND when you discover more about living creatures is that there are dozens of good ways. It's even true that there is no need to change at all. There are far more millions of simple jelly-creatures alive than there are of big animals like us. There they are, to this day. They live in the ground, in the sea, in ponds and rivers everywhere and even floating about in the air. It's really true that there are far more of them than of us. Some of them have not even grown the slightest flipper, let alone a brain. Their life may seem dull to us, but they are alive all right, which is what THEY want.

Then think of mice and elephants, they get on all right. Then there are all those absurd-looking creatures in the pictures. Then go on to creatures like apes and people. We get on all right.

How can it possibly happen that there are so many different sorts of creature?

So there's a question that used to puzzle me when I was young and it's a question which, now I'm grown up, I still don't understand. However, it's not just me that it puzzles but also a lot of other people.

There are millions of different kinds of places to live and so there are millions of different kinds of creatures to live in them. We can make pretty good guesses about some kinds of odd creatures: for instance, giraffes, angler-fish, seaweed fish, stick-insects (see if you can find him in the picture) and polar bears. Anyhow I'm glad that there are all these absurd beasts, not to speak of equally absurd plants. The world would be dull (which it isn't) if there really was one "best way".

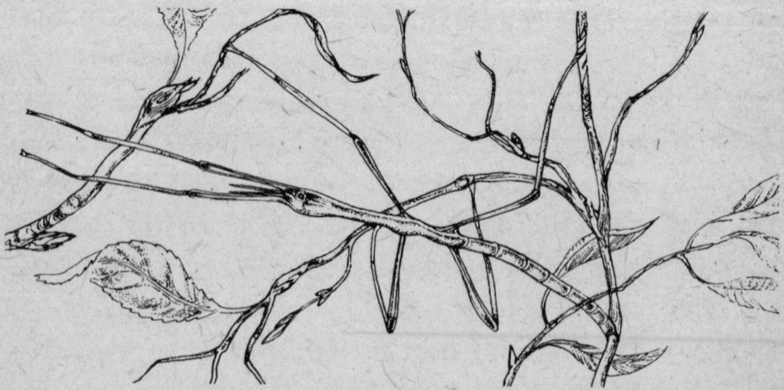

Fig. 22 — A stick-insect is hanging upside down from a twig. Once you find his head you can see him.

EXTRA CHAPTER

What is in this book was read to some children in two different schools when they had their NATURE STUDY lessons. This was before the pictures were ready. They asked a lot of questions. Asking questions is of course always the right thing to do when you are trying to learn about something.

A little girl of about seven, called Judy, wanted to know more about nerve threads (it's on page 000). She thought it was rather silly to need nerves for taking messages. She said:

"*Of course* the flippers knew when there was food coming, because they are part of the same creature as the tummy."

What I told her (when the teacher let me interrupt) is that your own hand or foot really and truly does not know "of itself". Nurses in hospital are always taught about this.

If a patient has had an operation, he is given an anaesthetic (sleepy stuff) so that he will not feel any pain. When he is put back to bed, if a nurse puts a hot-water bottle by his foot or by his side, she has to take great care not to have it too hot, and to wrap it up, because he would not know even if it was so hot that it was burning him. The anaesthetic would have prevented his brain and nerves from taking any messages at all, neither useful ones from his skin about the hot bottle, nor the useless ones about the pain of having an operation and stitches.

I once looked after a man who had had an operation on his head. When he had been put back to bed a nurse hadn't been careful enough; she had put a hot-water bottle at his feet without wrapping it up properly and the skin of one foot was quite badly burnt by the heat. When I helped to look after him he was quite well from the operation, but he had to stay in bed till his foot got better. He felt cross about this.

The anaesthetic had been breathed in through his nose and mouth, and it had done nothing to any part of his body except to his nerves and brain. So I could tell Judy for certain that feet and hands really don't feel of themselves.

Barbara, who was about nine, wanted to know how many miles of nerves she had? We said about a couple of miles.

In one lesson the teacher read the sentence about the dog. It's on page 000 and it's this: "Smell-nerve says to dog, 'There's a delicious bit of meat close to me' and quick as winking brain flashes back to teeth and tongue and throat — 'Snap it up and swallow it!' "

Two children thought that "Quick as winking" meant almost no time at all, so they asked if it would be as quick as lightning?

It would not. A message from the eyes or fingers of a person usually takes longer than a message from the eyes or nose of a dog.

(By the way, some people who are very clever in other ways, are quite slow at this seeing and doing quickly. So don't worry if you, or someone you like, are slow at it. This has nothing to do with the part of your brain that understands history or maths or the sort of things that are written about in this book.)

William, who was 8, wanted to know if white specks that he had noticed in raw meat were nerves? We said probably not, more likely specks of fat. But we agreed that in a mutton chop with its bone on you could often see a bit of the biggest nerve of all, the spinal cord that runs down inside the spine.

Fig. 23 — A chop. It was from looking at meat and weighing and measuring, that a lot was found out about how human beings work.

Luke asked: "Why do things hurt?" What he meant, the teacher felt sure, was, "Is pain any use?" The answer is that pain (hurting) is often very useful indeed.

It's a danger signal, and if a wild animal or a

person couldn't feel pain it would probably soon die of poisoning, or some wound or illness. Pain says: "Don't!" or "Look out!".

The man who had the operation for instance, got a burnt foot because for an hour or two, he could not feel any pain.

You and I rest a swollen foot and a dog runs on three legs and rests his hurt leg or his cut paw, but this is not because we are sensible and know that a hurt place often needs a rest so as to have time to mend, but because ordinary walking hurts. If it didn't we should probably forget and rush about as usual. So pain keeps reminding you that you'd better attend to whatever is wrong, and had better give the hurting part time to get better before you keep using it again.

But of course, pain can be a great nuisance.

William asked another question: "When is the heart formed?" We said that a human baby's heart can be heard inside its mother about four months before it is born.

Siân, who was about nine, wanted to know how many cells there were in her body *now*. We said millions and millions and millions.

Somebody wanted to know if all animals had two eyes, two legs, two arms and so on. We said "No" and to think about starfish or spiders.

After another lesson Pamela wanted to know why people think life began in the water? We discussed this but the teacher and I couldn't answer well enough off-hand, so, before next time, I asked a biologist who knows a great deal about these things.

He said that people thought that life must have begun in water because most creatures are made of flesh and bone or jelly and are very watery themselves. He told me that if I was thoroughly dried up I should be about a quarter the size and weight that I am. One of the chief things that skin is for, he said, is to prevent a person from drying and shrivelling up.

This, he went on, is so important that hardly any animals can live outside water or else very wet marshy places unless they do have a waterproof skin. You may have seen for yourself if you've been to the seaside how jelly-fish which have no proper skin dry up and die if the waves throw them up on to the sand.

But he went on to say that there are some very small single celled creatures, viruses and a very tiny sort of mite, that can get quite dry, then they float about in the air; but even they cannot grow and split or eat until, and unless, they get blown on to something wet.

To live out of water a creature will almost always need to grow a skin and the very simplest one-cell living things haven't got one.

A little girl of about seven (it was Pamela, who had asked about living in water) said: "So I was once like everything?"

We agreed that this was a good saying and very nearly true. We really were once like everything that is everything in our line, but we mammals were never much like insects.

Ann, who was eight, felt very sorry that she had shed her fur before she was born; and when the teacher came to the part about the fur-coated creatures keeping their babies inside them until they had been growing for some time, she said: "Yes, how nice! Then, if a lion ran after the mother she wouldn't have to go hunting about to find her baby."

Some of the children wanted to be quite sure if we meant that all the other mammals, such as tiger, began as jellies before they were born? The answer is, yes, they did.

A boy called Dai, wanted to know if people were gradually changing nowadays and if so, in what way? The answer to that is that nobody knows for sure, but that most people think that probably humans won't change very much from now on. "Why?" Dai wanted to know.

We said this might be because humans don't much need to change now. We know how to make tools and use them. Other animals change to suit the place they live in. Instead, humans wear clothes, build houses, make dams to prevent floods and change the places they live in in lots of ways to suit them.

Someone in the class wanted to know if we could manage even if another ice age came?

We said it was thought that we could keep warm all right, but might find it difficult to grow enough food.

Later on, one of the children who must have been thinking about an old nursery rhyme began to say:

> "What are little boys made of?
> Slugs and snails and puppy-dogs' tails."

Someone else joined in,

> "That's what little boys are made of!"

Then someone else went on with the bit about little girls:

> "What are little girls made of?
> Sugar and spice and all things nice
> That's what little girls are made of."

After that everybody laughed and wanted to know, "What are we all *really* made of?"

The teacher said: "How about this?"

> "Enough WATER to fill five two-gallon petrol tins.
> Enough FAT to make seven long bars of soap,
> Enough IRON to make one medium-sized nail,
> Enough SULPHUR to kill all the fleas on one dog,
> Enough CARBON to make the leads of 9,000 pencils,
> Enough LIME to whitewash one chicken-coop,

Enough PHOSPHORUS to make 2,200 match-heads."

And, the teacher went on, all this, and a few other things that also come in, could all be bought in the shops for less than two or three pounds.

But everyone agreed that even the greatest scientist or inventor could never manage to put it all together to make a person.

One of the children said: "But how does anyone know all that? No one can take a person to bits to find out? So how do you know?"

We said: "To start with, nowadays we know that our bodies are made of the same things as those of sheep and cows. That's known for a start. What flesh and bones are made of was found out by scientists who mostly made careful tests about 20 years ago.

First they minced and then they dried a certain weight of ordinary meat. Then they measured the water they'd dried out from that and from the bones as well. Then they separated out the fat and the minerals from the meat. Then they did the insides. They knew to start with, that all this would work out at about the same for the same weight of a human. The red meat of mutton, beef or pork is muscle and very much the same as your muscles. I told the children that my father used to tell me that cannibals used to talk about 'Long Pig' when they meant to eat someone, and that the cannibals, like the scientists, thought our muscles were more like pork than any other kind of meat.

A child said: "But I still don't see how scientists can tell about how much of everything there is in a person? Some people are fat, and some people are thin."

We said: "Just so. It depends on age too. You aren't grown up yet, so your bones aren't as heavy for the rest of you as they will be in ten years' time. I expect that's why the teacher only put the answer in a joking way to give just a good rough idea."

* * *

We have said a great deal in this book about animals being born, and very little about their dying, except about when they died to be food for some other creature.

We also said a great deal about animals growing long necks and so on — and very little about creatures whose children's children didn't go on with the good tricks that had been useful to their parents.

But this, not changing, and whole kinds of creatures dying out, happened often and often and often, and not just to the prehistoric creatures, but to lots of others. Some sort of forgetting is a pity, but some forgetting seems to be needed for learning new things, and some dying is certainly needed for being born.

Think about forgetting. Imagine animals whose children's children had not got the useful habit of not going on with growing anything that had stopped being useful? Imagine the sad life of a mole which still had eyes which got full of dirt, and still had long legs which got in its way when it was underground. Imagine too a woolly rhinoceros like the sort that lived in the Ice Age — but this one lived in the tropics now — how awful for the poor thing if it still kept its wool. If an animal or a person kept all the things that had been useful long ago to its ancestors, and never shed anything, that poor creature — what with having gills and wings and flippers and one thing and another — would be quite worn out with just growing up.

I wonder if you have ever thought of the idea that dying is also useful? It is a very good job, not only that the brontosaurus and the tyrannosaurus (whose names mean "thunder lizard" and "tyrant lizard") are all dead, but it is also a good thing that all kinds of quite harmless but very stupid creatures died out. There has to be enough room.

Every animal that dies or is killed makes room for a young one. With luck the young one may begin where the old one left off. It is the same with people. With every new lot of children there is a new set of chances of something marvellous being done or found out.

It is sad when an animal or a person dies without ever having had a chance. But when they have had a long life and learnt a lot, then it is all right that, at last, they should make room for a new, young, strong person or creature.

If this were not true, the world would be rather a sad place, and it would make most people feel unhappy to think of so many creatures dying, and of so many plants fading, for so many hundreds and thousands of years. But if we think that each lot that dies makes room for a new lot, with a new chance and fresh strength, than I don't think that it does seem sad.

THE END.

AFTERWORD FOR GROWN-UPS

THIS BOOK has made me very angry, not with its author, but with the remainder of the human race, and particularly the biologists, including myself, who did not write it. For it is the only book of its kind, so far as I know — which is a scandal. If every child in Britain were to read this book, their average expectation of life would probably be increased by about a year, for hygiene is applied biology, and you cannot act hygienically if you have not learned to think biologically.

As this book is the first of its kind, I should have to commend it even if it were rather bad, just as I should commend an animal which learned to live at the South Pole even if it were rather a poor sort of animal otherwise. As a matter of fact, however, the account of evolution given by Amabel Williams-Ellis strikes me as being more nearly correct than either of those two recently published by well-known scientific men. There are, of course, things that I should have put differently, and I should have stressed certain embryological facts which she has omitted. But then no child would have read my book.

There are one of two ideas in the book which might well appeal to a grown-up biologist. For instance, it is a very good account of embryology to say that we spend the first six months of our lives in playing at being extinct animals. For there is a certain lack of seriousness about the changes in bodily form which we undergo. Our gills are not very good gills, for example. We play at being fish, but it is only play. We are inadequate fish at four weeks, just as we are inadequate savages at nine years.

The opinion is widely spread that biology is unsuitable for young children. I do not agree with it. I knew the differences between the main types of animal, and the names of most of my bones, when I was seven, long before I knew any but common-sense physics or chemistry. And, in my limited experience, children find it just as easy to understand simple things about animals as about machines.

I hope that this book will run into many editions, in which its author will answer some of the questions which I should have asked if I had been lucky enough to read it as a child. If so, she may be encouraged to write the badly needed sequel, namely, HOW YOU WORK. I believe that she could do it, and I do not know of anyone else who could. If she is to be encouraged to do so, you should not only buy this book for your children, but induce your friends to do the same.

J. B. S. HALDANE

Dunn Institute of Biochemistry
Cambridge University
May 1928

JOHN BARBER